Maryland

by Patricia K. Kummer
Capstone Press
Geography Department

Content Consultants
Joe A. Swisher
author
The Complete Guide to Maryland Historical Markers

Betty Sue Swisher
Elementary school media specialist (retired)
Harford County, Maryland

CAPSTONE
HIGH/LOW BOOKS
an imprint of Capstone Press

C A P S T O N E   P R E S S

818 North Willow Street • Mankato, MN 56001
http://www.capstone-press.com

Library of Congress Cataloging-in-Publication Data
Kummer, Patricia K.
    Maryland/by Patricia K. Kummer.
        p.cm.--(One nation)
    Includes bibliographical references and index.
    Summary: Provides an overview of the Old Line State, including
its history, geography, people, and living conditions.
    ISBN 1-56065-680-8
        1. Maryland--Juvenile literature. [1. Maryland.] I. Title.
II. Series.
F181.3.K85 1998
975.2--dc21   97-40818
                                              CIP
                                              AC

Editorial Credits:
Editor, Cara Van Voorst; cover design and illustrations, Timothy Halldin;
    photo research, Michelle L. Norstad
Photo Credits:
Betty Crowell, 9
Thomas Fletcher, 40
William B. Folsom, 29
Joe Maguire, 20, 25, 26, 30
G. Alan Nelson, cover
Root Resources/C.Postmus, 4
James P. Rowan, 6
Lynn Sheldon Jr., 34
Unicorn Stock Photos, 33; Martha McBride, 5; Ted Rose, 5; R. Baum, 10;
    A. Gurmankin, 16; Andre Jenny, 23; Jean Higgins, 38
Visuals Unlimited/Bill Beatty, 14

Table of Contents

Fast Facts about Maryland

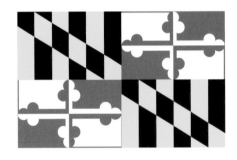

State Flag

Location: In the mid-Atlantic region of the southeastern United States

Size: 12,407 square miles (32,258 square kilometers)

Population: 5,042,438 (1995 U.S. Census Bureau estimate)

Capital: Annapolis

Date admitted to the Union: April 28, 1788; the seventh state

Baltimore oriole

Black-eyed Susan

Largest cities: Baltimore, Silver Spring, Columbia, Dundalk, Bethesda, Wheaton-Glenmont, Towson, Potomac, Aspen Hill, Rockville

Nickname: Old Line State
State bird: Baltimore oriole
State flower: Black-eyed Susan
State tree: White oak
State song: "Maryland, My Maryland," by James R. Randall

White oak

Chapter 1

The Star-Spangled Banner

On September 13, 1814, British warships moved toward Baltimore Harbor. The United States and Great Britain were at war for the second time in 30 years. This was the War of 1812 (1812-1815).

British forces started firing on Fort McHenry at dawn on September 13. Rockets lit the sky. Bombs exploded in the air.

The battle ended at dawn on September 14. The U.S. flag still flew over the fort. This meant the British had not captured the fort.

The U.S. flag still flew over Fort McHenry when the battle at Baltimore Harbor ended.

Francis Scott Key

The British captured and held some Americans on their ships during the battle. Francis Scott Key was one of them. Key watched the battle and hoped for a U.S. victory. Key wrote a poem when he saw the U.S. flag flying. He called the poem "The Star-Spangled Banner."

Within days, the poem became a song. People all across the United States sang Key's song. In 1931, "The Star-Spangled Banner" became the U.S. national anthem. An anthem is a song of national pride. Today, people stand and sing this song at many occasions.

Baltimore Harbor Today

Fort McHenry is now a museum. Visitors can touch the guns U.S. soldiers fired at the British.

The Star-Spangled Banner Flag House is near Baltimore Harbor. Mary Pickersgill sewed the star-spangled banner that flew over the fort in this house.

There are other places to visit along Baltimore's Inner Harbor. Fish and other water animals swim in the National Aquarium. The Maryland Science Center has exhibits about computers and space. Harborplace is an indoor shopping center. It has many shops and restaurants.

The *USS Constellation* is docked in the Inner Harbor. This warship was the first ship built for the U.S. Navy. It served the U.S. Navy from 1797 to 1945. Visitors can tour the ship's living areas and battle decks.

The USS Constellation is docked in the Inner Harbor.

Chapter 2
The Land

Maryland is a mid-Atlantic state. It lies in the middle of the East Coast along the Atlantic Ocean. Maryland's lowest point is along its coast. This point is at sea level. Sea level is the average level of the ocean's surface.

Maryland is also a southern state. Three other southern states border Maryland. They are Delaware, Virginia, and West Virginia.

Washington, D.C., borders southwestern Maryland. Pennsylvania is north of Maryland.

Chesapeake Bay
Maryland has 3,190 miles (5,136 kilometers) of coastline. Most of this coastline lies along Chesapeake Bay. The bay separates eastern Maryland into the Eastern Shore and the Western Shore.

Most of Maryland's coastline lies along Chesapeake Bay.

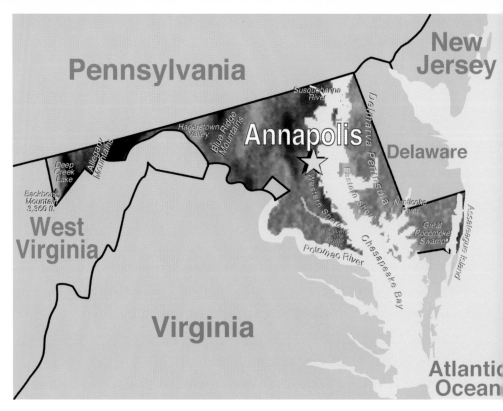

Many Marylanders live near Chesapeake Bay.
Baltimore is Maryland's largest city and chief
port. Baltimore is on the Western Shore of
Chesapeake Bay. Annapolis is on the Western
Shore, too. This city is the state capital.

Several islands lie in Chesapeake Bay.
They include Kent, Tilghman, Smith, and
Bloodsworth Islands.

Rivers

Many Maryland rivers run into Chesapeake Bay.
They include the Susquehanna, Nanticoke, and
Patapsco Rivers.

The Potomac River also flows into Chesapeake Bay. The Potomac forms Maryland's southern border with West Virginia and Virginia.

Coastal Plain

The Coastal Plain covers eastern Maryland. This lowland includes parts of the Eastern and Western Shores. The Eastern Shore is part of the Delmarva Peninsula. A peninsula is an area of land that sticks out from a larger area of land. Peninsulas are surrounded by water on three sides. The Delmarva Peninsula includes parts of Delaware, Maryland, and Virginia.

The Pocomoke Swamp is on the Eastern Shore. Rich farmland lies on the Eastern Shore, too. Fruits and vegetables grow well on this land. The Western Shore also has good farmland. Farmers grow tobacco there.

Piedmont

The Piedmont is west of the Coastal Plain. Piedmont means at the foot of a mountain. Mountains rise west of the Piedmont.

Wild ponies live on Assateague Island.

Maryland's Piedmont has low, rolling hills. Crops grow in river valleys in the Piedmont. Dairy cattle graze on the Piedmont's grasses.

Appalachian Mountains and Valley

Some of the Appalachian Mountains rise above western Maryland. Two mountain ranges form Maryland's part of the Appalachians.

The Blue Ridge Mountains are just west of the Piedmont. Thick forests cover these slopes. Sometimes a blue fog hangs over the forests. This gave the range its name.

The Allegheny Mountains stand far to the west. Backbone Mountain is in the Allegheny Mountain range. Backbone Mountain is Maryland's highest point. It rises 3,360 feet (1,024 meters) above sea level.

Hagerstown Valley lies between these two mountain ranges. There are farms and apple orchards in this valley.

Wildlife

Black bears roam the western mountains. Off the Atlantic Coast, wild ponies live on Assateague Island. White-tailed deer, red foxes, and gray foxes also live in the state.

Chesapeake Bay is home to many kinds of shellfish. Clams, oysters, and crabs live there. Chesapeake is an Indian word. It means great shellfish bay. Diamondback terrapins also live in the bay. These turtles are mascots for the University of Maryland. A mascot is something meant to bring good luck to a team.

Climate

Maryland has warm, humid summers. Its winters are usually mild. The western mountains have cool temperatures year-round. They also receive the most snow.

Chapter 3

The People

Maryland has the 19th-largest population among the states. More than 81 percent of Marylanders live in or near cities. About half of these people live in and around Baltimore. Baltimore is the nation's 14th-largest city.

Some suburbs of Washington, D.C., are in Maryland. These suburbs are called the Capital Region. Many Marylanders live there but work in Washington, D.C.

Maryland is one of the fastest-growing eastern states. Each year, many people settle in Maryland. They come to Maryland from many places throughout the world.

European Ethnic Backgrounds
About 70 percent of Marylanders have European backgrounds. They are the state's largest group.

Most Marylanders live in or near cities.

Some Marylanders are relatives of early English settlers. Others are relatives of early German settlers who farmed in northwestern Maryland.

African Americans

The first Africans came to the land that is now Maryland in the 1630s. They worked for seven years as servants. Then they gained their freedom.

By the 1650s, Europeans brought Africans to Maryland as slaves. The slaves worked on tobacco plantations. A plantation is a large farm. Slavery ended in Maryland in 1864.

Today, African Americans make up about 25 percent of Maryland's population. Many African Americans moved to Maryland from other states. Others recently arrived from African countries like Nigeria. Maryland has a large population of Nigerians.

Asian Americans

Asian Americans are Maryland's fastest growing group. They make up about three percent of the population. Many of their families came from China, India, and Korea.

Montgomery County has a large Indian American community. In 1992, Kumar P. Barve was elected to Maryland's legislature. A legislature is a group of people that makes laws. Barve became the first Indian American elected to a state legislature. Barve lives in Montgomery County.

Hispanic Americans

About two percent of Marylanders are Hispanic Americans. Many live in suburbs of Washington, D.C. Some live in Baltimore.

Maryland has the third-largest population of Salvadorans among the states. Other Hispanic Americans came to Maryland from Puerto Rico and Mexico.

Native Americans

By 1750, few Native Americans remained in Maryland. European settlers had forced them off their land.

Today, about 13,000 Native Americans live in Maryland. Most are Lumbee, Cherokee, or Piscataway people. They live mainly around Annapolis and Baltimore.

Chapter 4

Maryland History

People first lived in Maryland about 10,000 years ago. By the 1600s, about 5,000 to 7,000 Native Americans lived there. They included the Nanticoke, Patuxent, and Susquehannock people. These Native Americans lived along the Nanticoke, Patuxent, and Susquehanna Rivers. The rivers are named for them.

English Colonists
In 1632, England's king said a nobleman named Cecil Calvert could set up a colony in the Maryland area. Calvert's title was Lord Baltimore. The city of Baltimore is named after him.

Calvert was a Roman Catholic. Catholics could not worship freely in England. Calvert said people of all Christian religions could settle in Maryland.

Maryland's first English colonists lived in St. Mary's City.

He believed all Christians should be able to worship as they pleased.

In 1634, the first English colonists arrived in Maryland. They bought a village from a group of Native Americans. The colonists named this village St. Mary's City.

Many Maryland colonists grew tobacco. Some built plantations. Plantation owners kept African slaves to do the work on their plantations.

Revolutionary War

The colonies mainly governed themselves. But in the 1760s, Great Britain increased its control of the colonies. Great Britain's government placed high taxes on goods colonists bought in the colonies. This led to the Revolutionary War (1775-1783).

Maryland helped the other 12 colonies win the war. Ships made in Chesapeake Bay were used to capture English warships. Baltimore served as the country's capital from December 1776 to March 1777.

After the war, Annapolis was the U.S. capital for about a year. Congress met in Annapolis and approved the treaty that ended the war.

The Seventh State

In 1788, officials from Maryland signed the U.S. Constitution. Maryland became the seventh state to join a new country called the United States. Annapolis was named the state capital.

In 1791, Maryland gave some land to the U.S. government. The nation's permanent capital was built on that land. It became Washington, D.C.

Annapolis was the U.S. capital for about a year after the Revolutionary War.

Growth in Maryland

Roads, canals, and railroads crossed Maryland by the 1830s. They connected Maryland with other states.

Baltimore's shipyards built clipper ships. These fast sailing ships carried goods around the world.

Slavery and the Civil War

By 1860, the issue of slavery divided the nation. The Northern states did not allow slavery. Maryland and other Southern states did. But few Marylanders owned slaves. More free African Americans lived in Maryland than in any other state.

Eleven Southern states left the United States in 1860 and 1861. They formed a new country called the Confederate States of America. The two countries fought each other in the Civil War (1861-1865).

Maryland's legislature sided with the United States. In 1864, Maryland adopted a new constitution that ended slavery in the state. About 50,000 Marylanders helped the Union win the Civil War. About 22,000 Marylanders

Baltimore shipyards built clipper ships.

fought for the Confederate military. In 1863, the U.S. government freed all slaves throughout the nation. In 1865, the Confederate States of America surrendered.

Growth after the War

Thousands of Europeans came to Maryland after the Civil War. They took jobs in the

The military trained thousands of soldiers at Fort George Meade.

state's factories. Many freed slaves from other states also moved to Maryland.

Some Marylanders built boats called skipjacks. Fishers use these boats to catch oysters in the Chesapeake Bay. Workers canned and packed the oysters in Crisfield.

In the late 1800s, Baltimore became an important city. Businessmen started libraries and museums. A businessman named Johns Hopkins donated money for a university and a hospital.

World Wars and the Great Depression

In 1917, the United States entered World War I (1914-1918). The military trained thousands of soldiers at Fort George Meade. The army tested weapons at the Aberdeen Proving Ground.

The nation experienced a bad financial period during the Great Depression (1929-1939). By 1932, more than half of Maryland's factories had closed. Thousands of workers lost their jobs. The U.S. government helped with the New Deal program (1933-1939). The program created government jobs for people.

In 1941, the United States entered World War II (1939-1945). Maryland factories built planes and warships. These planes and warships helped win the war.

From Segregation to Integration

Since the 1800s, laws in Maryland and other southern states segregated African Americans and European Americans. Segregate means to keep apart. The laws were called Jim Crow laws. Jim Crow laws said these people should live separately but equally. The laws established separate neighborhoods, restaurants, and schools.

In 1954, the U.S. Supreme Court said sending minority students to separate schools was illegal. Maryland integrated its schools faster than any other southern state. Integrate means to make places, services, and goods available to people of all races. Children of all races began attending the state's public schools together.

Maryland also passed the South's first integrated housing law. This law allowed people of any race to live in any neighborhood.

Cleaning Up Chesapeake Bay

Waste from farms, cities, and factories entered Chesapeake Bay. It polluted the bay for many years. The waste killed many of the fish and shellfish that lived in the bay.

In 1985, Maryland started a program to clean up Chesapeake Bay. Today, less untreated waste flows into the bay. Since 1995, workers have placed about 300 million oysters in the bay. Marylanders hope Chesapeake Bay can again become a great shellfish bay.

Marylanders hope the Chesapeake Bay can again become a great shellfish bay.

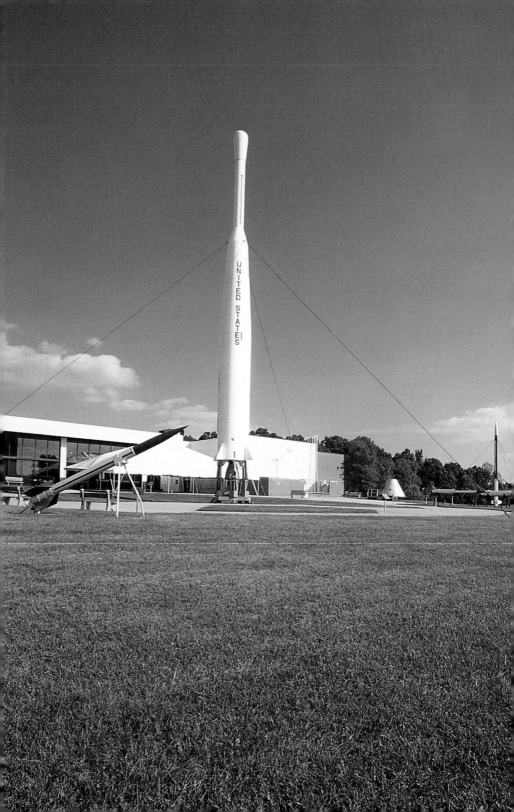

Chapter 5
Maryland Business

In 1995, Maryland's workers had the fourth highest incomes in the nation. About 80 percent worked in service industry jobs.

Today, Maryland's leading service industries are government, trade, and tourism. Manufacturing, farming, and fishing are other important Maryland businesses.

Government Work

Several U.S. government offices are in Maryland. They are near Washington D.C. The National Institutes of Health is in Bethesda. It is a research center for medicine and diseases. The Goddard Space Flight Center is in Greenbelt. The center is a space-science laboratory.

The Social Security Administration's headquarters is in Baltimore. The administration provides financial help for older and disabled

The Goddard Space Flight Center is in Greenbelt.

people. The U.S. Naval Academy is in Annapolis. The academy trains students to become officers in the U.S. Navy.

Other Service Industries
Tourists spend about $6 billion each year in Maryland. Hotels, resorts, and museums receive much of this money.

Trade is also important in Maryland. Baltimore is the nation's 17th-busiest port. Many products from other countries enter the United States through Baltimore Harbor. Maryland's businesses also ship goods to other countries from the harbor.

Manufacturing
Packaged foods are Maryland's leading manufactured products. McCormick and Company makes spices in Hunt Valley. Canneries pack seafood and vegetables along the Eastern Shore.

Electrical goods are another leading product. Black and Decker makes power tools in Baltimore. Chemicals such as soaps and paints are also made in Maryland.

Agriculture
Chickens are a major farm product in Maryland. Farmers on the Eastern Shore raise most of these

The U.S. Naval Academy trains students to become officers in the U.S. Navy.

chickens. Milk is the state's second-leading farm product. Frederick County's dairy cattle produce the most milk in the state.

Flowers, shrubs, and fruits are Maryland's leading crops. Soybeans, corn, wheat, and tobacco are important, too. Maryland's orchards produce apples. Farmers also grow tomatoes.

Fishing

Fishing produces more than $50 million for Maryland each year. Fishers catch crabs, clams, and oysters from Chesapeake Bay. They catch bluefish and shark from the Atlantic Ocean.

Chapter 6

Seeing the Sights

V isitors find much to see in Maryland. They learn about the state's history in Maryland's cities and towns. They have fun in Maryland's recreation areas.

Western Maryland

The Savage and Youghiogheny Rivers flow through far western Maryland. Brave visitors go white-water rafting down these rivers. White-water rafting is steering a small boat through fast-moving water.

Deep Creek Lake is Maryland's largest lake. The lake is a reservoir on the Youghiogheny River. People make reservoirs when they build dams. Water from a river backs up behind a dam to form a lake. Large resorts lie along the lake's shores.

Cumberland is east of Deep Creek Lake. The Transportation and Industrial Museum is in

More than 23,000 soldiers were killed, wounded, or reported missing in a Civil War battle at Antietam.

Cumberland. Visitors learn about Maryland's early roads, canals, and railroads.

Antietam National Battlefield is southeast of Cumberland. Soldiers fought an important Civil War battle there in 1862. More than 23,000 soldiers were killed, wounded, or reported missing in this battle. Today, visitors can walk or drive through the battlefield.

The Capital Region

The Capital Region is near Washington, D.C. It includes Frederick and Prince George's Counties.

Catoctin Mountain Park is in northern Frederick County. Park visitors enjoy hiking and cross-country skiing. Camp David is in the park. U.S. presidents often take their vacations at Camp David.

Andrews Air Force Base is in Prince George's County. U.S. presidents take off from this base in Air Force One. Air Force One is the official airplane used by U.S. presidents.

Southern Maryland

St. Mary's City is in far southern Maryland. This city was Maryland's first capital. Today, the city has an outdoor museum. Marylanders

Bethesda, Rockville, Silver Spring,
Wheaton and Potomac are suburbs
of Washington D.C.

reconstructed the colonial capitol and the *Dove*.
The *Dove* is one of the ships that carried the
first Catholic colonists to Maryland.

Calvert Cliffs State Park is north of St.
Mary's City. The park's cliffs rise 120 feet (36
meters) over Chesapeake Bay. Visitors can look
for shark fossils. A fossil is the remains of an
animal or plant that lived many years ago. This
region was once part of the ocean.

Visitors to the Babe Ruth Birthplace Museum learn about the New York Yankees' famous home-run hitter.

Central Maryland

Annapolis is in central Maryland on Chesapeake Bay. It is north of Calvert Cliffs. Annapolis has been Maryland's capital since 1694. The State House was built in 1772. This is the oldest capitol in the nation that is still in use.

The U.S. Naval Academy is also in Annapolis. The navy trains officers there. The academy's grounds and museum are open to visitors.

Baltimore

Baltimore is also in central Maryland. The World Trade Center building in Baltimore is at the Inner Harbor. Visitors view Baltimore from the center's 27th floor. Exhibits show Maryland products that are sent to other countries.

Baltimore is famous for its neighborhoods. Some neighborhoods have miles of brick row houses. These houses are connected to each other. There is no space between them. Many of the row houses still have their original shiny, white marble steps.

The Babe Ruth Birthplace Museum is in a row house. Visitors learn about the great home-run hitter who played for the New York Yankees.

Pimlico Race Course is also in Baltimore. Each May, the Preakness horse race is held there. The winning horse receives a blanket of black-eyed Susans. The black-eyed Susan is Maryland's state flower. The winning horse's owner receives about $750,000.

The Eastern Shore

The Chesapeake Bay Bridge links the Eastern Shore with the rest of Maryland. St. Michaels is south of the bridge. Visitors can tour the Chesapeake Bay Maritime Museum there.

Blackwater National Wildlife Refuge is south of St. Michaels. Bald eagles and peregrine falcons live there. Both birds are endangered. Endangered means in danger of dying out.

Ocean City is far east of the refuge. This city lies on the Atlantic Ocean. Each summer, about 8 million people visit Ocean City. They sunbathe, swim, fish, and go boating. Some enter sand-sculpting contests. They build huge sand castles.

Each summer, about 8 million people visit Ocean City.

Maryland Time Line

About 8000 B.C.—People are living in Maryland.

A.D. 1600s—Several Native American groups including Susquehannocks, Nanticokes, and Patuxents are living in Maryland.

1608—English captain John Smith explores Maryland's Chesapeake Bay.

1632—King Charles I of Great Britain gives Maryland to Cecil Calvert, Lord Baltimore.

1634—English colonists arrive with Governor Leonard Calvert, Cecil Calvert's brother, and found St. Mary's City.

1649—Maryland passes the Toleration Act, which gives religious freedom to all Christians.

1694—Annapolis becomes Maryland's capital.

1775-1783—Maryland joins the other colonies in the Revolutionary War and wins independence from England.

1776-1777—Baltimore is the U.S. capital.

1783-1784—Annapolis serves as the U.S. capital.

1788—Maryland approves the U.S. Constitution and becomes the seventh state.

1791—Maryland gives up land along the Potomac River for the U.S. capital at Washington, D.C.

1814—Francis Scott Key writes "The Star-Spangled Banner" during the War of 1812.

1861-1865—During the Civil War, Maryland remains in the Union and adopts a new constitution that ends slavery in the state.

1876—Johns Hopkins University opens in Baltimore.

1952—The Chesapeake Bay Bridge opens.

1954—Baltimore's public schools are desegregated.

1983—The Baltimore Orioles win baseball's World Series.

1987—Barbara Mikulski becomes Maryland's first female U.S. Senator; Kurt Schmoke becomes Baltimore's first African American mayor.

1992—The Orioles' new baseball park opens. The ballpark is called Camden Yards.

Famous Marylanders

Benjamin Banneker (1731-1806)
Mathematician and scientist who helped survey
and draw up plans for the city of Washington,
D.C.; born in Ellicott City.

John Wilkes Booth (1838-1865) Actor who
shot and killed President Abraham Lincoln;
born near Bel Air.

Margaret Brent (1600-1671) Maryland's first
female landowner; asked Maryland's assembly
for the right to vote but was turned down; born
in England and moved to St. Mary's City.

Frederick Douglass (1817?-1895) A slave
who escaped to freedom and then founded *The
North Star*, an anti-slavery newspaper; born in
Tuckahoe.

Francis Scott Key (1779-1843) Lawyer and
poet whose poem "The Star-Spangled Banner"
(1814) became the U.S. national anthem; born
in the area that is now Carroll County.

Thurgood Marshall (1908-1993) Lawyer who argued before the Supreme Court for the end of segregated schools (1954); became the first African American Supreme Court justice (1967-1991); born in Baltimore.

Edgar Allan Poe (1809-1849) Writer famous for writing scary poems and stories; born in Massachusetts, spent his early writing years in Baltimore; died in Baltimore.

Cal Ripkin Jr. (1960-) Baseball player for the Baltimore Orioles; set a major league record in 1995 for playing in 2,132 consecutive games; born in Havre de Grace.

Babe Ruth (1895-1948) Baseball player who set many home-run records; one of the first five players elected to the Baseball Hall of Fame (1936); born in Baltimore.

Harriet Tubman (1820?-1913) A slave who escaped to freedom (1849) and helped more than 300 other slaves escape through the Underground Railroad; born in Dorchester County.

Words to Know

anthem (AN-thuhm)—a song of national pride

clipper ship (KLIP-ur SHIP)—a fast sailing ship

endangered (en-DAYN-jurd)—in danger of dying out

fossil (FOSS-uhl)—the remains of an animal or plant that lived many years ago

integrate (IN-tuh-grate)—to make places, services, and goods available to people of all races

Jim Crow laws (JIM KROH LAWZ)—laws saying that African Americans and European Americans should live separately but equally

plantation (plan-TAY-shuhn)—a large farm

row houses (ROH HOUZ-uhz)—a row of houses connected to each other

sea level (SEE LEV-uhl)—the average level of the ocean's surface

segregate (SEG-ruh-gate)—to keep people of different races apart

skipjack (SKIP-jak)—a small sailboat made for harvesting oysters

white-water rafting (wite-WAW-tur RAFT-ing)—steering a small boat through fast-moving water

To Learn More

Fradin, Dennis Brindell. *Maryland*. From Sea to Shining Sea. Chicago: Children's Press, 1994.

Kent, Deborah. *Maryland*. America the Beautiful. Chicago: Children's Press, 1990.

Kent, Deborah. *The Star-Spangled Banner*. Chicago: Children's Press, 1995.

Thompson, Kathleen. *Maryland*. Portrait of America. Austin, Tex: Raintree Steck-Vaughn Publishers, 1996.

Internet Sites

City.Net Maryland
http://www.city.net/countries/united_states/maryland/

State of Maryland
http://www.state.md.us/

Travel.org Maryland
http://travel.org/maryland.html

Useful Addresses

Babe Ruth Birthplace Museum
216 Emory Street
Baltimore, MD 21230

Banneker-Douglass Museum of African American Life and History
84 Franklin Street
Annapolis, MD 21401-2738

Fort McHenry National Monument and Historic Shrine
East Fort Avenue
Baltimore, MD 21230

Maryland State Board of Tourism
217 East Redwood Street
Baltimore, MD 21201

United States Naval Academy Visitor Center
52 King George Street
Annapolis, MD 21402

Index